LOVE, LIFE
and the
LEGION

LOVE, LIFE
and the
LEGION

ALLEN STOKES

To order additional copies of this book, contact:
Xlibris
800-056-3182
www.Xlibrispublishing.co.uk
Orders@Xlibrispublishing.co.uk
756078

Contents

Acknowledgments

I wish to thank the following people because without them this book would not have been published

My aunty Liz

Shenton

Paula

Rdh stokes

You know who you are

THANK YOU ALL

Nan you're always in my thoughts

Come and goings

People come and people go
When it's a friend my mood is low
Soon I hope it will be my turn
Then the midnight oil I can burn
Now I'm well enough to leave
My marching orders is what I'm waiting to receive
Which I hope I will soon get
Then by the grace of god I shall leave
But at the moment I feel caught in a net
Or like a fish on the end of a line
I can go out at 8 then back at nine
That's morning and night by the way
I always try to do what they say
But at the end of one day
I'll be on my way
And so will you
Just tow the line that's all you gotta do

Is this the end?

What if the light you see at the end?
From whence you're ready to ascend
Is the light of a new beginning?
The light of a room for the newly living
A reborn future
You're a baby again ready for nurture
You'll forget the life you've been living
Forget all you've been given
You'll forget all about the life you've left
And start all afresh
Always a new beginning never a final end
Take a different road go round a bend
A chance to turn a corner and make amends
Enter a new world of silicon v r, and micro chips
And so forever from life's cup you'll sip
Continue on the path of life death life
Wife children death children wife
Always receiving a new and better life
But remember don't repeat the same mistake thrice
Dai jar vous, you might think it's the same
But as a reborn you're playing a different game
A curtain over your mind
So you can't see the past inside
Different beginning new people same end
Never ever to meet god
But just to get a new life a new bod
Because if this was the end
It would drive me round the bend

Good news

Good news chases away the blues
I'm getting a flat although I need to join a que
I'm being taken off my section three
Although when well we will have to see
I really can't wait freedom at last
Time to move forward and put away the past
At the moment I'm on lime
Just doing my time
I go out for four hours a day
And on a Sunday I go to church to pray
Well it is good for the soul they say
Got the news yesterday so over the moon today
I've waited and worked so hard
Even a medium secure had marked my card
But I prayed and fought prayed and thought
And I'll make sure if I go bad I'll never get caught
Time to move on
And make amends with my son Jon
He's everything to me he's my whole life
Although I never ever took a wife
But now it changes no more strife
It's time to live my life
Not exist but live
As I have so much to give
So now today it's time to live my life

Life on Hazel

A new day
A new beginning
So happy and positive I'm almost singing
For days like this Oh do I pray?
A winter's day with the sun shining
It just shows every cloud has a silver lining
No more pining
No more sighing
I even ignore the people who are lying
As even a little white lie
Can make you cry
Shouting stamping their feet
No wonder I can not sleep
A door bangs here a scream there
But they don't care
Can I have my meds?
Strap them down and inject them instead
No-one's well and consistent
But who will really listen
The staff try the patients lie
I pray to the lord
Please not another day on Hazel ward

Life on the ward

Sitting at a table playing cards
Betting on the horses
Or playing charades
Waiting for lunch
Giving a mate a playful punch
Or playing pool
Laughing nearly fell off my stool
Then being told to keep my cool
Getting the hospital spiral
Waiting for my poetry to go viral
Listening to the nurses moan about their day
Waiting for a patient to have his say
Doing woodwork at O't
Or making an ash tray out of clay
Listening to the f word over and over again
Gets on my wick it's such a pain
So all this considered I view myself sane

Poorly

The noise on the ward goes up and down
Silence is never the only sound
A scream here a shout there
Sounds so much like an angry bear
Nurses running to and fro
Why does it always have to be so
The panic alarm rings in my ear
I go to my room and shed a tear
Oh for just one peaceful night
I hear a shout get out of my sight
Banging doors stamping feet
So I huddle under my bed sheet
Until the morn when it's nice and calm
Then it all starts again on the funny farm
Take 5 mins have a fag
I'm going home now let's pack a bag
I never ever want to feel so low
The thing to give up is that nasty blow
Never again will the devil take my reins
As I am in control of my own brain
Take the pills swallow them down
Don't be silly of course you know how
It's now time to live life to the full
Out on town on the pull
Then my life will be so much better
That's the reason I write this remembrance letter

Friends Poem

When it's all gone to pot
And your head is shot
Just when your being driven round the bend
Always remember you've got a friend

A shoulder to cry on
Someone to lift that ton
And carry it for you
Just because they love you too

The art of war

The art of war is so raw

Kill or be killed?

That is the question

Run or hide?

With a hail of bullets

They get swept aside

Glide through the jungle?

Hide in the desert?

As wide as the ocean death is my potion

It heals

It feels

It kills

it's my pill not my drug

The clock is ticking

How do you tell someone special your time is nearly up?
And that it may not be long until your drinking from deaths cup
The clock is ticking
And from this world I am slipping
Slowly painfully on my way
But I hope and pray I'll be allowed to stay
I may not have led a good life
And I do leave behind a son but not a wife
Do I really deserve to die?
And when in a coffin will I lie
But for another chance I do pray
Please god im not ready to leave I say
But don't shed a tear please don't cry
Cause to heaven one day all our souls must fly
As my corps lays in a coffin
Just lying there slowly rottin
All I ask you don't stand by my grave and cry
As it may just be a short goodbye

Allen Stokes

The junky prayer

Our father who art in rehab
Heroin be thy name
Thy dealer come
Thy hit done
On earth then straight to heaven
Give us this day our daily hit
And forgive us our misses
As we forgive those who miss us
Lead us into temptation
And deliver us our fix
For thy is the dealer
The powder and the money
For ever and ever
Amen

The Only Fun I get

It's good to get time off the ward
Without it I would be bored
I only get four hours
So the rest of my time I take showers
You make a friend
Then they get moved it drives me round the bend
If I'm not in the shower I'm folding paper
What a bloody caper
Spend the rest of the time on the internet
And when I go out I like to have a bet
Walk in with twenty
Walk out with forty
Playing the roulette I know it's naughty
But a win's a win
I don't even care that it's a sin
Well not really
And I'm doubling up as you can see
So I'm going to say this really clearly
Don't judge me let me be
As the only fun I get
Is my daily bet

The true price of war

Sent to war as a youth
In unit armed to the teeth
Nothing but sand not a tree not a leaf
Aged only nineteen
I shouldn't of seen wot I've seen
And part of an elite fighting force
Not the British army but the foreign legion of course
Always assemble for roll call
Being told you can die with honour
There's body bags for you all
Aim your rifle pull the trigger
The feeling of being a god getting bigger and bigger
But at the end of the day can I take a life
Knowing he might have a son and or a wife
But if it's him or me
I won't have a choice you see
Now that I am one of France's sons
Told to write a last letter home to your loved ones
Your mom and dad kids and or wives
Its true wot I say I tell no lies
I was that scared I even wet the bed
Please believe me its true what I've said
And for this cause I willingly bled

Thinking of You

I think of you every day and night
Right up till first and last light
You're on my mind and in my heart
It makes me sad that we are apart
But one day soon
I'll make your heart swoon
And I hope you will be mine
As my life would be so fine
I found you now I'm not letting you go
Because I want to love you so
You deserve the best
And will get nothing less
My heart I give
For you I live

Voices

The voices inside my head
Totally take over my mind
They don't tell me to be kind
They tell me to kill instead
Grab a knife take a slice
Eat a human it tastes real nice
To torture and to kill
Oh what a thrill
When they are there I have no free will
Then when the paranoia kicks in
That's when they really win
What did that bloke just say?
Go on make him pay
Kick him stab and punch
Ha ha now for a free lunch
I'll put the rest in the freezer till later
I'm my own cook my own little waiter
Then off to the nuthouse for a good two year
And I won't even shed a single tear
My time for discharge is coming near
Which means I'm better and going home
And the reason I'm writing this poem

War never ends

The last bullet fired doesn't end a war
As you always remember your tour
It never ends with the last battle or fight
It goes on in your mind every night
To go to war is exciting or so it seems
But night after night. Have you heard my screams?
I dream and scream dream and scream
This is now my night or so it seems
I've killed people I don't even know
Who would make me? Us? Do so
Of friendly fire there's no such thing
Screaming is the tune by which I sing
Aim straight aim true
Don't look at your target shoot straight through
Don't pull but squeeze that trigger
The targets close getting bigger and bigger
I may have laughed twas just a nervous snigger
But now at night inside I cry
And with every passing day I die
A lot of sorrow a lot of regret
One legionnaire even had a bet
On how many he would get
I cannot move on I cannot live
As my actions is what I need to forgive
I was young but now am old
The man I killed his body is cold
I'll live to regret it till my dying day
And one day a bigger price I'll pay

Watching

Watching the bustle
Watching feet shuffle
Watching the landscape
Watching the world in its dormant state
Watching the feeding birds
Watching the cows huddle in herds
Watching the frost creep across the grass
Watching the ice that looks like glass
Watching the wind rustle the trees
Watching the winter flowers without the bees
Watching the sun shine so bright
Watching as it spreads it's still warm light
Watching the clouds creep across the sky
Watching the day say goodbye
Watching all from a window on the ward
Now off to give thanks to the lord

Winter from the Window

Sitting at a table looking out
Watching the world go round and about
A wonderful beauty is the frosty grass
Just watching as the birds fly past
It looks and feels so icy and cold
The trees could tell a story they are that old
The leaves have fallen from the trees
And lying dormant are all the bees
The sun still shines so big and bright
Making the frost glisten a beautiful white
Like diamonds scattered in the grass
And the ice like shards of broken glass
Watch your footfalls watch your steps
With mother nature a balance is kept
Soon the sun will shine
And the weather will be t-shirt fine
Till then it looks like all has died
And going out is where I draw the line
Because its bloody cold outside

Flying in the clouds

Look up to the sky so bright
And see the clouds so beautiful and white
Imagine flying among them so high
The fluffy white around you as you fly
The sun above so close so hot
Reminds me of being safe and warm in my cot
As you rise you feel lovely and warm
Totally ignoring a passing storm
Hear the angels play a soft tune
Stay, enjoy, and don't come down too soon
With grace they pluck gently on the harp
Hey! Watch out that mountaintops really sharp
Feel the wind rushing past your ears
As your eyes fill with ecstasy tears
Now down you come land nice and soft
And never forget your time aloft

Don't Do Never

Don't look at me with those eyes
Don't take the mick about my size
Don't shout at me for the whole world to hear
Don't push me away bring me near
Don't make me shed a single tear

Do love me like you used to
Do only say it if its true
Do tell me you love me
Do its with me you want to be
Do say you'll marry me
Do spend the rest of your life with me

Never hurt me
Never another should you see
Never alone should we be
Never will I love another
Never go running to your mother
Never ever go running into the arms of another

Getting There

If words were life
If you could talk your way out of strife
If you can love and still live your life
If you can take a woman and make her your wife
If you can keep hold of all you've got
If you can without losing the lot
If you can dampen the fire inside you
If you can help a friend too
If you can live a life of happiness
If you can do it without too much a mess
If you can live a life with less
If you can do it without losing soul
Then you'll have lived a life whole

Happy birthday

A happy birthday to my baby
My one and only beautiful lady
We may be apart now but soon to be together
Then when we are we will be apart never
I send you my love on this your special day
I hope you listen to all that I say
I love you now and always will
Even in death I'll love you still
We talk on the phone we talk on skype
You make my heart beat faster
You make me hype
Please my darling forget the past
As this … our love is built to last
My darling I love you know and forever
We will be apart again. Never
So now once again I wish you a happy birthday
On this you're very special day

He's waiting and always chasing

There's a man called death
He's there when you take your last breath
Always waiting
Never straying
When you're on his list
You will see a thick mist
He's come to collect
His job he won't neglect
Swings his scythe
Cuts your life line
To end your life
Pay the ferryman
No named Stan
Off you go to join your family clan
Up to heaven or down to hell
Depends if your soul to the devil did you sell
Tuppence on your eyes
A hole dug to size
Now here you go on your own
Down the last road you've ever known
Maybe off to paradise city
Where all the girls are pretty
Or into the fires of hell
There for eternity you will dwell
There for eternity you will scream and yell

I am me

Passion fills my body
Like the morning chorus fills the emptiness of the soul
Like water that fills every crevice
Like the root that stretches far from the tree
It ripples like a stone in a lake
Spreads far and wide like the ocean waves
I'm as high as a mountain
As deep as a valley
People follow me like rocks dragged by a glacier
I attract like a magnet
Stronger than any other
My mind and body know no bounds
I am me

I'm just asleep

Don't stand by my grave and weep
All our cherished memories please keep
There's nothing there but an empty hole
I've seen the ferry man and paid my toll
I'm only sad that I've left you behind
You were so truthful loving and kind
Now I ascend to heaven full of grace
Needing no more to fill my nose full of base
As the high I feel now is above any other
And waiting there is my Nan my dad my mother
Every night ill stand by your bed
Please my sweet don't worry your head
Oh my darling please don't cry
This is but a short goodbye
And as I said please don't weep
Just look at it as an infinite sleep

I'm not mental

Living with an illness is so very hard
It's as if someone has marked your card
Anxiety depression and stress
A case where friends know you best
Doing things for the first time
Totally shaking inside
You get a smile you know the kind
The one that says that's a pity
But really it's pretty shitty
Don't tell me you understand
Because it's not you who's stuck in the sand
Please look at me
Tell me who not what you see
I'm a person just like you
We all suffer not just a few
Look me in the eyes
Don't give me the sly smiles
It's not your pity we want
Its equality that we need that we hunt
We are the same you and me
And that hopefully you will all one day see

Is this the end?

What if the light you see at the end?
From whence you're ready to ascend
Is the light of a new beginning?
The light of a room for the newly living
A reborn future
You're a baby again ready for nurture
You'll forget the life you've been living
Forget all you've been given
You'll forget all about the life you've left
And start all afresh
Always a new beginning never a final end
Take a different road go round a bend
A chance to turn a corner and make amends
Enter a new world of silicon v r, and micro chips
And so forever from life's cup you'll sip
Continue on the path of life death life
Wife children death children wife
Always receiving a new and better life
But remember don't repeat the same mistake thrice
Dai jar vous, you might think it's the same
But as a reborn you're playing a different game
A curtain over your mind
So you can't see the past inside
Different beginning new people same end
Never ever to meet god
But just to get a new life a new bod
Because if this was the end
It would drive me round the bend

Living with PTSD

To the devil I've sold my soul
Into the eternal fire it goes
Pay the ferry man then off I'll go
Why I did it I do not know
But a life of crime
Was the first sign
I hate myself for what I've done
But at least I haven't condemned my only son
The steps of heaven is not my way
Live a life like mine and down you go they say
I've killed a man so now I'll pay
I wear the badge of a single tear
I really hope I'm making this clear one single shot to the head
I could argue it was war not me, and yet I bled
I bleed every night, scream till I wake
Getting not even one nights break
It was war and orders I can plead
But punishment is still what I need
We were only there cause of one mans greed
And every night I watch him bleed
They say treatment is all I really need
It's not very nice is PTSD
But will it get better? I'll have to see
The longer I do live the more of me I give
Forgive yourself is what they say
And for me they promise to pray

Nan

I lost my Nan a year today
She was there every day
Then one day she was gone
Not even time to say goodbye to her grandson
I miss her still
And always will
Especially when I say her name
Now life just aint the same
With you gone my Nan Kathleen
You helped me through life made sense of what I had seen
And where I had been
She taught me right from wrong
Made me. Me made me strong
She looked at me stern
When I wouldn't learn
She was always there
Listened when I needed to share
One of The only ones who really did care
When my parents beat me
Safe and well she would always keep me
Away from harm
Safe and calm
Lovely and kind
Nan your always in my thoughts and on my mind

Lust- trust

Lust

Trust

Desire

Fire

Heart apart

In the bath

Oh at last

Cold shower release the power

Now

POW

Never

Forever

Young

Old

Age never told

Lies behold

Cold heart

Always apart

Warm and loving

Heart string tugging

I want you

I need you

When things go wrong

Together too long

Cupid you want to sue

Then look for someone new

Nightmares of Memories

Sitting here in the middle of the night
Biding time till first light
Twas a nightmare that first awoke
A nasty voice that spoke
I woke sweating and screaming
Why am I always dreaming?
A lots happened in my life
From beatings to abuse and basic strife
Hit with a bar stabbed with a knife
A few times now I've nearly lost my life
I had it all and lost the lot
Now nothing have I got
I've been stabbed beaten and shot
And nearly put someone in the cooking pot
All these come back and haunt me
A future without I cannot see
I move around run away and flee
Please will I ever be free

Nothing in life is free

Breakfast lunch and tea
Nothing in life is free
As you can see
You want the home the car the washing machine
Your money your wages are never seen
Paying for a child by a previous wife
You'll never have enough to enjoy life
Paying of a loan no money left I hear you groan
Buying a house or car
Hoping your child will be a star
Living off immoral wages
Taking life by stages
Then deciding to go straight
Doct pay cause you woke up late
Build a garage build a fence you can
cause you've saved every pence
Now someone comes and steals the lot
And insurance you haven't got
Now start again and buy the same
All because you've lost the lot

Regrets

Evil thoughts
Come to naught
Flesh eating dreams
Cannibal so it seems
Locked away
Hospital stay
Section three
Meals for free
Hard drugs
Bed bugs
Lose the lot
Live in a squat
On the street
Use girls on the beat
Meet a beautiful dove
But incapable of love
Freezing feet
Lost my teeth
No respect
Someone's guest
Is all regrets

Something in Life for All

A mountain to climb
A passage in time
Womb to grave
Scared yet brave
Street to home
No life set in stone
Got it all lost the lot
Aim your rifle take the shot
Had a life lost my wife
Hearing voices
A life full of choices
Tick tock
Goes the clock
Birth then death
Run out of breath
Son or daughter
Cut your life shorter
Young then old
It's all been sold
Sanity vanity totally insane
If you had the chance would you do it again
Same wife or a new romance
Sliced wrist broken neck
Pay a debt bounce a check
Say goodbye
To heaven you fly
Death was waiting
And always chasing

Relief

Boring
Waiting
Sitting
Hoping
Playing pool
OT's like going to school
Walking around
Wearing a halo
Can I go to Tesco?
Watching TV
Putting on a DVD
Ward round
Drs Review
Head spinning round
Washing clothes
Watching late shows
Jeremy Kyle? Get some style
Increased leave
Now you can breathe
Reading
Eating
Told your leaving
Then relief
Now come on hurry
Saying thanks to staff
To friends a sorry
But it's your turn soon
Then your brain goes boom
With relief

Arabian Nights

It's so cold in the desert at night
The sky so dark yet beautifully light
Because the moon shines so bright
Not a cloud in the sky
All the stars shine their light
You stand there shivering in the brightest darkness
It's so wonderful yet weird
The dark so close so near
Standing in the shadow of the desert night
Sand as far as the eye can see
You feel so alone as alone can be

Awake Again My Brain Screams in Pain

Memories are like poison in the brain
I can't sleep due to the nasty dreams
No wonder I go a bit insane
I wake up crying and/ or screaming in the night
And stay awake right up till it gets light
No wonder I have trouble sleeping at night
Even that don't half give me a scare
Even talking about it
Really makes me feel like shit
Some say "But it's only a nightmare"
Sometimes it's good to share
And although I shout although I swear
And my screams shatter the night air
I've been to war
And they say talking is the cure
Makes me feel like hitting them with a big bloody door
But I don't and I won't
Help is all they're trying to give
So a good life I can live
Even when people see me cry
They must think I'm a div
But about one thing I cannot lie
I'd do it all over again
Even put up with the pain
If I was still young and had the chance
Until my dying day I'll always and say the same

Beatings

Angry
Banging
Slapping
Beatings
Sleeping
A kick here
A punch there
The belt
A welt
A bruise
I lose
Worry
Sorry
Don't start
I come apart
Children's home
Thrown stone
Slap
Snap
Broken bone
Then I left home

Bristol Sights

Bristol sights
Bristol nights
Bristol lights
Bristol girls
Watch them twirl
For their smile
You'd walk a mile
For their laughter
You would keep them happy ever after
The way they make you feel
Their sexy appeal
The glint in the eyes
The oh not you again sighs
Their clothes
The shows
Strike a pose
There she goes
Where you can be you
And I can be me too
After all's said and done
It's nothing new
So why not come
Come to Bristol it's all true

Broken

Waiting boring
Sleeping snoring
Nightmares do I share
Crying Weeping
My heart is bleeding
Tick tock round the clock
Time for bed eyes of lead
I cry I shake until I wake
Look ahead never back
A life a mind begins to crack
Sharing the past
Please don't let it last
I can't lie I want to die
Awake asleep
Memories I keep
Remembering talking
I'm always walking
Secrets I keep
Take a peek
You're in my heart
We're worlds apart
Memories to share
I'm in despair
I slay I hit
I pray cos I feel like shit
In God we trust
As I know I must

Go away take it away
I cry I shake I pray
I cry I pray
No more to say
So in my mind I pray

Control

Don't look at me with those big brown eyes
Don't give that sexy smile
You know I'll love you till the end of days
I don't care what my best friend says
You know you drive me totally wild
You say you wanna marry and have my child
But there's no taming this wild bear
I love you and you know I care
Go on take me on if you dare
You may lose but you may win
At least then we won't be living in sin
But if all goes well
What will be no-one can tell
All I do know is you will win

Crimes against society

Crimes against society
is total insanity
having to put up and shut up
that's why were locked up
can't go out and about
just scream and shout
and no longer does a copper just give you a clout
locked up in nick
your cell mate is a PRICK
eat breakfast before you leave
out the gate now you can breath
the screws shout "you'll be back"
"yeah well I hope you get the fucking sack
Waiting for a train or bus
You may think you've got life sussed

Self-Harm

It's painful it hurts
It's sinful it burns
Makes me feel good
Boils the blood
But the body's a temple
That's why it's sinful
Makes me feel well
In my mind rings a bell
It relieves stress
I wish I hurt less
Makes the voices go
Helps when feeling low
I've tried everything else
That's why I do this to myself
No one understands why
So I do it on the sly
I pray to God
To forgive what I do to my bod
My face chest arms and legs
Please stop my friend begs
But they don't understand
It's what the voices demand
Now I'm left with scars
So I cover up in clubs and bars
Take a blade bring it close
It's not enough just one dose
Again and again now no more head pain

Allen Stokes

The voices leave so now I can breathe
Until they come back
But tools of the trade I do not lack
You may think I'm a Burk
But the pills don't work

Death Awaiting

Age before you
Birth behind
Stick it where the sun don't shine
A world created by God
But a life that's mine
When you die there's nothing but black
You're going down into a little body-sized crack
You've lived your life
And now been given the sack
You leave behind a sexy little wife
No more worries no more strife
No more being told don't do that with your life
Wrinkled and old
No more will you feel the cold
You're now in death's grip
Fell down the stairs with a broken hip
No longer from life's cup will you sip

Crimes against society

Crimes against society
is total insanity
having to put up and shut up
that's why were locked up
can't go out and about
just scream and shout
and no longer does a copper just give you a clout
locked up in nick
your cell mate is a PRICK
eat breakfast before you leave
out the gate now you can breath
the screws shout "you'll be back"
"yeah well I hope you get the fucking sack
Waiting for a train or bus
You may think you've got life sussed

12 months alone

On the street young and all alone
And someone one day threw me a bone
He gave me a place to stay
But every night nasty dreams would blow me away
In these dreams I was being abused
In those dreams I was being totally used
He would make me a coffee before bed
Unknown to me down a path I was being lead
He would lace my coffee with a drug
Then make sure I was tucked in nice and snug
This went on for a whole year
Unknown to me he was trying to make me queer
Until I caught him on one of those nights
Then I really did knock out his lights
I did a runner never turned back
I had given this bloke his place the sack
Never ever looking or going back

A cure for snoring

I woke with a start
My head felt like it was coming apart
In my mouth was the barrel of a gun
My first thought was this is real not a bit of fun
And in the darkness all I could see
Was someone standing over me
The figure laughed a horrible laugh
And put his gun away
That'll stop him snoring I heard the darkness say
The Sargent thought for a bit of fun
In my mouth while I'm asleep he would place his gun
I still wake up screaming in the night
With him his gun the only things in sight
But when I turn on the bedroom light
There's no one at all in sight
This dream I can't ignore and believe me now! I no longer snore

A smile is an upside down frown

Walking around or playing pool all day long
Writing poetry or listening to a song
Being told I'm doing good or totally wrong
The problem is on the ward the day is so long
Boring watching the clock as they say
Waiting for another passing day
Hanging around until bed
All day long my eyes feel like lead
Cause I know if I sleep during the day
I won't sleep at night
Well that's what my Nan used to say
For others its different all work no play
With us we play as others work
We play up we play down
And get written about if we frown
Or act like a clown
But soon that frown will turn upside down
And change in to a smile when I'm away from here
It don't have to be far just a mile
For that frown to become a smile

All I want for xmas

All I want for Christmas is to go home
That's why I'm writing this poem
To be off my section three
And like a bird totally free
So I've asked the doc
He said hmmm maybe we will see
But when things are getting tough
And I'm feeling rough
These days in hospital I will remember
And I am not coming back ever
The friends I've made I won't forget no not ever
No more will I burn my arm cut or sever
No more will I shout or scream
No more nightmares oh I beg I plead
I'm eager I know
Or it may seem so
I really do want to get out
I could scream I could shout
But I won't

Alone

In a world, full of people, I feel so alone
In a room, full of people, I feel on my own
If I was barley or wheat I would be sown alone
And alone I would be grown
One drop of water is all I would be given
If I was a tree I would have one branch one leaf
If anyone was to die I would never experience grief
I'm one biscuit in the barrel one apple on the tree
One fiver in a homeless man's wallet
If I was a leg one of a pair I would be just one knee
I wouldn't be an ocean just a sea
But I am being told to mingle, fit into society
But for me that's like climbing ab solid smooth glass wall
And even if I could it would be just too tall
I hear your gasps I hear your shock
In the 1500si would be placed in the stocks
Well here is the answer to the question you ask
To fit in has always been my task
The reason I don't fit into society
Well that's easy I've got ptsd

Anger

The feeling first starts in our boots
Then through every muscle as up our legs it shoots
And as our body tenses shakes and starts to quake
It's so intense we feel all our bones are about to brake
The adrenalin courses through our veins
As they carry it around our body to are brains
We get the high and our fists and toes are clenched
Our blood boils and so with sweat we are drenched
I've already decided not to run but to fight
Making me get to this point was not very bright
As the red mist encloses my brain
I can feel my self going totally insane
I look you straight in the eye
Already in my mind I'm saying good bye
My muscles bunch
My shoulders hunch
My eyes are now covered bye a cloud of red
Even before the second punch lands its over
Even before you hit the ground you're dead.

< 19 >

Allen " the big fella" Stokes

.

Watching

Watching the bustle
Watching feet shuffle
Watching the landscape
Watching the world in its dormant state
Watching the feeding birds
Watching the cows huddle in herds
Watching the frost creep across the grass
Watching the ice that looks like glass
Watching the wind rustle the trees
Watching the winter flowers without the bees
Watching the sun shine so bright
Watching as it spreads it's still warm light
Watching the clouds creep across the sky
Watching the day say goodbye
Watching all from a window on the ward
Now off to give thanks to the lord

Printed in Great Britain
by Amazon

79104602R00038